Mars, the Roman god of war.

PRITCHETT & ASSOCIATES, INC.

The
MARS
PATHFINDER
Approach to
"Faster-Better-Cheaper"

What does your job have in common with a mission to Mars? Actually, more than you might think.

You're probably not tackling a project as dramatic as landing on another planet. But chances are you're being asked to do things differently. To pick up speed, upgrade quality, and lower costs.

You're not alone. "Faster-better-cheaper" is the market battle cry being sounded around the world. Organizations everywhere are in a competitive race—trying to do things quicker, improve output, and do it all for less money.

Let's look at a particularly fascinating example.

On July 4, 1997, the Jet Propulsion Laboratory (JPL) landed the Pathfinder spacecraft on the surface of Mars. Perhaps you were one of the fascinated millions watching TV or logging onto the Internet to see the Sojourner rover roll onto the rugged terrain of the Red Planet. People the world over—young and old, from all walks of life—watched in wonder as the little machine explored the rocky surface for clues to the evolution of Mars and hints to whether life could have existed there.

While the Viking mission had landed two spacecraft on Mars back in 1976, there were several remarkable differences with Pathfinder. First, the Pathfinder mission was completed much faster—in three years instead of six. Second, Pathfinder was actually three spacecraft in one, with much better technology and engineering, and including the first robotic explorer to roam the surface of another planet. Finally, the Pathfinder mission was 15 times cheaper than the previous Viking mission.

Faster…better…cheaper.

How was the small band of JPL scientists, engineers, and support team members able to accomplish this feat? And why did this particular mission capture the imagination of hundreds of millions of people around the world? Several reasons. But according to Flight System Manager Brian Muirhead, the key success factor was *people*.

Pathfinder displayed creative engineering. It achieved scientific breakthroughs. But Brian is quick to point out that those innovations were possible only because of the people involved.

"Faster-better-cheaper" doesn't just happen. It takes an eye for innovation. A determined effort to discover new, more powerful approaches. We must become explorers…adventurers…more willing to experiment, and much better at managing risk.

We interviewed Brian Muirhead to study the success of the Pathfinder project. We spent days listening to him describe the spirit and creativity of the Pathfinder team. His insights are condensed here into 13 lessons which serve as living proof that "faster-better-cheaper" works in deep space as well as it does on Earth. Each lesson is followed by an example from Brian's experience, giving us direct insight into how this mission to Mars was so successful.

We invite you to start practicing the Pathfinder approach outlined here. You'll come to believe more in possibilities and less in limitations. You'll find the courage to stretch for great achievements. Finally, you'll become more innovative, and you'll create some of the most meaningful, exciting, and fun experiences of your life.

"Exploration and discovery are, as they always have been for humanity, the pathways to our future."

—NASA

PATHFINDER: *A brief biography*

For four full decades, people all across planet Earth have watched in awe as the National Aeronautics and Space Administration (NASA) and California Institute of Technology's Jet Propulsion Laboratory (JPL) escaped the pull of gravity to explore the reaches of outer space. Their achievements were ours. We've taken great personal pride in what they've proven about the human race. They've demonstrated that we have astounding potential. That our creativity and pioneering spirit can take us to the far reaches of our universe. That we need not limit ourselves to living within the bubble of our own planet's atmosphere.

Just as they have shown us how to extend our reach—how literally to shoot for the stars—they now are showing us how to change. They've given us a compelling case study of how to innovate, adapt, take risks, and achieve. It's captured here in the story of Mars Pathfinder.

Let's pick up the story in 1992, when Daniel Goldin took over as NASA's leader. The cold war was over. It was a time of heavy-duty budget cuts. Governmental agencies were shrinking, and at the same time seeking to get more bang for the buck. Also, the space agency's relationship with politicians and the general public—its "customers"—was rather strained. There had been some high-profile, expensive failures. For example, the $1.6 billion Hubble Space Telescope needed glasses. The Galileo mission to Jupiter had failed to deploy its large antenna, greatly reducing its ability to transmit data to Earth. Then in early 1993, the billion-dollar Mars Observer suffered a mysterious failure while trying to enter Mars' orbit—possibly a propulsion system failure—and was never heard from again. Things had to change.

At the same time, across the corporate world there was a push for "faster-better-cheaper," and that became the mantra for NASA as well. Goldin's concept for a fresh approach to space exploration came to life in the Discovery Program. This "faster-better-cheaper" idea meant increasing the number of planetary missions, and doing them for less than $150 million a piece (in 1992 dollars). These projects were to take no longer than about 36 months to implement. If they took longer or cost more, Goldin vowed he'd pull the plug.

This brings us to Mars Pathfinder, the first approved mission in NASA's new Discovery Program. It was designed to test a low-cost, innovative way of landing a spacecraft on another planet. The project team also was supposed to deploy a free-ranging rover as a technology demonstration. Finally, a key objective was to gather the first direct data ever obtained on the makeup of Martian rocks, so we could begin the detailed understanding of Mars' geology and evolution.

Why Mars? As the planet most like Earth, it has an atmosphere, polar caps, and possibly large amounts of water underneath the surface. Basically, it's the only other planet in our solar system likely to have harbored life, and the only one that someday might support human expeditions or even colonies.

As *Wired* magazine states, everything about the Pathfinder mission was "small, youthful, low rent, inventive, and fast." JPL spent a mere $200 million designing, building, launching, and landing Pathfinder with the microrover Sojourner. Another $50 million were spent on an unmanned Delta rocket to kick it into space from Cape Canaveral. As *Wired* points out, this was "pocket change compared to the $3 billion (in 1992 dollars) of the Viking project to Mars," completed some twenty years earlier.

Pathfinder launched from Cape Canaveral Air Station on December 4th, 1996. After a quick seven-month journey targeted directly toward Mars, it arrived at the planet on July 4th, 1997.

Instead of going into orbit as Viking had done, Pathfinder sliced straight toward the surface, screaming through the thin Mars atmosphere at over 16,000 miles per hour. Five miles up and two minutes before impact, a parachute was deployed to slow the craft. When Pathfinder had descended to 1,000 feet from the ground, a 19-foot tall raspberry-like bubble of four airbags inflated to cushion the lander for impact. Four seconds later, deceleration rockets brought the contraption to a dead stop in midair. Then the 800-pound lander dropped to the surface of Mars from a height of about 65 feet.

It was a perfect "bounce down," slamming onto the dusty and rock-strewn surface of Mars at about 35 miles per hour. Pathfinder bounced 50 feet high, then 23 feet, finally rolling and bobbling to a stop—right side up.

Once the lander came to a stop, the airbags deflated and retracted. The lander's three petals opened like a flower, and its camera began taking magnificent color pictures of the Martian terrain. The next day, after one of the collapsed airbags that was obstructing the ramp had been pulled clear, the little Sojourner rover crawled off the lander and left its cleat marks in the powdery soil of Mars. The 24-pound microwave-oven-sized rover busily set about its scientific work—taking pictures, studying rocks and soils through its alpha proton x-ray spectrometer, and sending us an amazing amount of new data about Mars.

It had taken 44 months from start to touchdown. Compare that with the 1976 Viking mission to Mars that took about seven years and peaked at over 2,000 NASA and JPL staff and contract personnel. Pathfinder's project team peaked out at about 320 people.

The "faster-better-cheaper" approach proved wildly successful. The Pathfinder lander was expected to operate for 30 days but lasted almost three times that long. The Sojourner rover was supposed to work for only seven days. But it wandered about, exploring, discovering, and sending data to Earth for almost three months. In the process, four times more data than expected—some 2.6 billion bits—were returned from Mars during the mission.

When Pathfinder landed and began sending pictures of Mars back to Earth, people all around the globe found personal inspiration in what NASA and JPL had achieved. It truly was a human event experienced the world over. During the first 30 days alone, the Internet registered over 450 million hits on Mars Pathfinder websites around the world. People everywhere have been stirred by this inspirational story about innovation, high aims, high risk, and the achievement of spectacular results.

Pathfinder was last heard from on September 26th, 1997, and JPL officially stopped trying to communicate with the lander about a month later on November 4th. In more ways than one, Pathfinder lived up to its name. It blazed a trail for future missions, setting a new standard of excellence for deep space exploration under NASA's now proven mantra of "faster-better-cheaper."

"The Independence Day triumph inaugurated a bold new era of planetary exploration by proving that 'better, cheaper, faster' missions, as NASA Administrator Dan Goldin puts it, can succeed. 'This is a new way of doing business,' Vice President Al Gore said in a congratulatory phone call to JPL on the Fourth, 'and its [validity] is being borne out by your dramatic success today.'"

—*Newsweek*, July 14, 1997

Chapter 1

Spectacular night launch of Mars
Pathfinder on December 4th, 1996.

The first image from the surface of Mars.

Set goals that make you stretch.

Set goals that make you stretch.

The Mars Pathfinder project demonstrates the power of great expectations. This team of people set out to achieve spectacular results, and that very ambition called forth the creativity and commitment their goal required.

The most important aspect of how to begin deals with where you expect to end. So point yourself toward a dramatic destination. Wrap your efforts around a fine cause—some high challenge—knowing you'll feel a sense of true achievement when you cross the finish line.

when you finish school   Just as you did

Why? Because high aspirations fire the imagination. When we aim our efforts toward something truly special, it stimulates us to think on a completely different scale.

Stretch goals force us to go beyond gradual improvements. Pushed to operate on a completely different level, we have to come up with strategies and techniques that greatly extend our reach. This triggers our competitive spirit, and turns on our creativity.

It's usually not enough for the goal just to be hard to accomplish.

It also needs to be compelling. Dramatic. An emotional turn-on.

Then it takes on an element of fun. It becomes sort of a contest or

game. The effort that this calls for feels different. It's not at all easy, but

while it's hard, it's enjoyable. And we're hooked by the challenge.

This sense of mission touches us on an emotional level, tapping into

our own rich pool of creative energy reserves. *REMEMBER BOOT CAMP.*

Innovation and commitment come more naturally when you aim high,

when you're operating with a clear, singular sense of purpose...with

sizzle! Then, even if your day-to-day responsibilities don't have much

pizzazz of their own, you'll still be spurred to do great things because

your efforts are connected to the drama and significance of the

larger mission. *To BECOME A GOOD LEADER, HUSBAND, EMPLOYEE, AND A MAN OF GOD.*

BRIAN: In late 1992, the NASA Associate Administrator for Space Science, Wes Huntress, called JPL and said, "I want you guys to do the first mission of an exciting new program called Discovery." We knew what that meant. It was a whole new kind of program. The budget was fixed at $171 million, with an additional $25 million allocated later for the rover. The schedule also was fixed—three years from start to launch. Then, just to make it really sporting, he said, "And I want you to go to Mars and land on the surface."

After we caught our breath, we sent back our reply. "We'll give it our best shot." We all knew, of course, that technically, a Mars lander mission would be a very difficult job. But to do it within the constraints of the Discovery Program made it significantly more challenging. I was in the elevator when some guys were coming down from a meeting about Pathfinder, and I heard them say, "This is crazy. There's no way these guys are going to pull this off." Over and over again throughout the development of the project, we heard, "You're not going to make it."

The mission objectives were simple:

- Demonstrate a reliable, low-cost system for placing a science payload and mobile rover on the surface of Mars.

- Demonstrate the mobility and usefulness of a microrover on the surface of Mars.

- Return new engineering and scientific data on the nature of the Martian atmosphere and surface.

But to meet these objectives it would take a special team of people. Because we were going to do things differently, it attracted innovators and some renegades. It was a major challenge, so it hooked the risk-takers and the people with a competitive spirit. And because it was a mission to Mars it hooked everyone else.

NASA had thrown us a mission that looked almost impossible, and a lot of smart people were betting against us. I don't know how many people really consciously thought about it at the time, but this became a make-or-break mission for JPL. Without knowing it, we had become the poster child for "faster-better-cheaper."

Early, 1994 blueprints of Pathfinder's lander and rover.

Let limitations guide you to

Chapter 2

Pathfinder entered Mars'
atmosphere at 16,400 mph.

The parachute opened at
mach 2.2.

The impact on Mars' surface
was at 35 mph.

Total time from entry to
touchdown was 4.5 minutes.

Pathfinder's Sojourner rover, named for Civil War-era abolitionist Sojourner Truth, was the first robotic explorer to roam another planet's surface.

breakthroughs.

Let limitations guide you to breakthroughs.

Constraints and limitations can be more of a blessing than a curse. They force you out of standard operating procedure. They call forth cleverness, push you toward simplicity, and give rise to elegant solutions. Demanding conditions also influence you to focus your efforts on what's most important.

The Pathfinder team didn't resist, give up, or argue for an easier set of conditions. They accepted the challenge. They were willing to go with the constraints.

So what's the lesson here? When you're feeling cornered by tough, seemingly unrealistic circumstances, maybe the situation is pressuring you toward a breakthrough solution. See where the limitations take you. Look for the trap door of innovation, the escape route of creativity that can solve your dilemma. Yield to the demands. Let them push you toward a unique answer that solves your problem.

Don't waste your time and energy struggling to change the conditions. Accept them. And apply your imagination toward finding a new and better way within these constraints.

Approach the situation as if it were a riddle...a routine way of looking

at it won't work. You've got to give it a twist. Go at it from a new

angle, and find the secret passageway that can serve as the solution.

More often than not, you'll end up using a simplified approach. And

despite the demands you're working under that you thought would

make things harder, you'll end up with a solution that turns out to be

easier.

As Plato said, "Necessity is the mother of invention."

BRIAN: The constraints were daunting. NASA said, "We want you to do a planetary mission to Mars and we want you to do it for a fixed price—$196 million." This budget was less than the production cost of the movie *Waterworld*. We were being asked to do a major NASA mission for the cost of a Hollywood movie. "Well, at least our ending will be better," we joked. We also had to do the job in three years, which was about half the time of recent planetary mission developments.

These were very challenging constraints. But because they were so challenging, they drove innovation. They drove the creativity of the team. We knew we had to find different new ways to do business, and that was exciting.

The constraints drove innovation in two major areas—the first was in the use of new technologies. We developed and flew over 25 new or significantly reinvented technologies, ranging from the flight computer to the rover to our famous airbags.

The second area of innovation was in how the team operated. For one thing, the team was lean. We talked about being only "one-deep," because we ran so lean. But I remember Cindy Oda, a member of the Operations team, commenting, "It's better to be understaffed than overstaffed. Being understaffed, you're a little uncomfortable and people get more creative. They find other ways to do what they're asked to do."

The Pathfinder project gave people an opportunity to grow professionally and personally. Someone would see a job that needed to be done and would say, "I can do that." Instead of letting a skilled, experienced person go, we'd let them grow into new jobs. A manager would say, "Looks like your job is almost done. Here's a new opportunity. It's going to require you to stretch, but you're ready for it." People saw that happening a lot and liked it.

You always got better employees this way. They became more versatile, more valuable to the next project, because they had broader experience. And they were personally much more motivated. They were excited about the opportunity to learn new things. They could see their value and the contribution they were making. They weren't stuck in a niche. They could grow into new jobs. We gave people the opportunity to take on additional responsibilities, to show themselves capable, and they did the rest.

Deliberately choose to do things

Chapter 3

differently.

Pathfinder developed new capabilities to produce and interpret 3-D stereo images. These images were essential to understanding the surroundings and driving the Sojourner microrover.

Deliberately choose to do things differently.

Don't wait for innovation to happen by accident, make it happen on purpose. Be very intentional about this.

The Pathfinder team set out with a charter to develop new, more powerful ways to explore our solar system. From the outset, the Jet Propulsion Laboratory team operated with the intent to innovate. It was a clear and conscious choice.

This kind of front-end decision, backed up with real action, sets the course for creativity. The key word, of course, is action.

Many organizations see the need for innovation but fail to act on that insight. They don't really change the way they do things. Maybe they're ready and willing to embrace breakthroughs that could bring a "faster-better-cheaper" solution, but they do little to make it happen. And since fate or dumb luck offers lousy odds for innovation, these outfits don't make much creative headway.

You must be willing to abandon your existing approaches. You must actively search for new solutions. And in making these new moves, it's not enough merely to improve on your established practices, such as

trying to do "more of the same" faster, better, and cheaper. The idea is

not just to intensify your same old efforts. It's to do something entirely

different.

Decide to go exploring, and then move on that decision. Experiment.

(BETTER KEEP IT — YOUR BOSS MAY WANT IT BACK)

Throw away the rulebook, do things differently, and see what you

discover.

BRIAN: It was actually in our charter: Develop new ways of doing business. Our first mission objective was to demonstrate a simple, low-cost system for placing a science payload and mobile rover on the surface of Mars. This required us to conceive and implement a very different approach to doing business in almost every area.

Doing things differently meant throwing out the rulebook. We had to be very creative about how we did things. But we didn't really *talk* about being innovative, creative, or inventive. It was a given. It was what we were about...what we had to do. It was an undercurrent that people just understood and accepted.

But we had to be smart about doing things differently. We used our knowledge and experience to keep the practices that we knew worked, while inventing new approaches to replace those we knew wouldn't work. We developed a list of new ways to do business that we felt were essential to our success, then presented those ideas for review. Many people were skeptical. There had been a lot of talk about new ways of doing business, but few had been successful. Many took an "OK, prove it" attitude, so we set out to do just that.

One of the first new things we decided on was to take the fast lane to Mars. There're a couple of ways to get there, but we followed the fast seven-month trajectory directly into the atmosphere of Mars at 16,400 miles per hour. This was the first time anybody had ever attempted to enter Mars' atmosphere directly. The Viking missions had gone into orbit before entering the atmosphere. The Pathfinder entry was going to be fast and furious. We really had to thread the needle to survive entry. If we came in too shallow, we'd skip right out like a stone on water. If we came in too steep, we'd burn up. It took a remarkable team effort. The navigation team told us where we were and where we needed to go. The propulsion and the attitude control teams determined how long we needed to burn and in what direction. The final maneuvers we had to carry out were make-or-break. If someone screwed up, we could blow it completely, and everyone knew it.

As it turned out, we took a 300,000,000-mile trip and arrived right on schedule...within a few seconds of when we'd planned to land.

We chose to do things differently, but we did things smart. And we followed through. People always asked at reviews, "You guys had to cut corners, didn't you?" And we'd tell them, "No, we actually added tests." That's typically where missions run into trouble. They run out of time and/or money, so they begin cutting out tests, the only thing left to cut. But we didn't. We knew testing was key to our success and found ways to keep testing, right up to landing day.

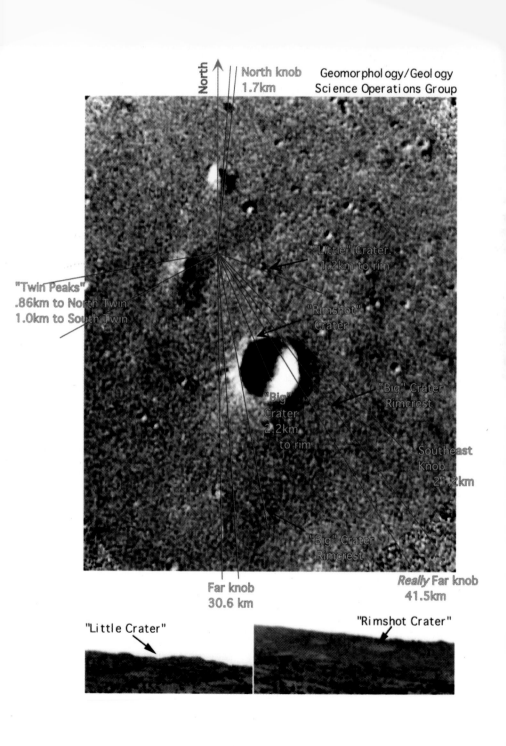

North

North knob
1.7km

Geomorphology/Geology
Science Operations Group

"Little" Crater.
1.2km to rim

"Twin Peaks"
.86km to North Twin
1.0km to South Twin

"Rimshot"
Crater

"Big"
Crater
2.2km
to rim

"Big" Crater
Rimcrest

Southeast
Knob
21.2km

"Big" Crater
Rimcrest

Far knob
30.6 km

Really Far knob
41.5km

"Little Crater"

"Rimshot Crater"

Discipline
creativity.

Chapter 4

Highly innovative outfits like the Pathfinder team operate according to a peculiar, unique set of rules. They break tradition. They violate cultural norms. But it's not an "anything goes" kind of culture. These work groups are demanding, hard on themselves, sometimes downright exacting.

Each person working on Pathfinder was expected to align with team goals and contribute. Everybody had a "deliverable"—a clear, tangible output he or she had been assigned—positioning the individual to contribute in a meaningful way.

Creativity was encouraged. But new ideas had to pass rigorous tests and respect all three parts of NASA's "faster-better-cheaper" emphasis. The team operated with a strong sense of discipline. The project was not some reckless, self-indulgent exercise where people could operate much as they pleased.

Of course, innovative organizations do take lots of risks. They experiment, test out ideas, and "push the envelope." For this approach to work, however, you need standards and self-discipline in the outfit.

Informed, calculated risk is one thing—sloppy mistakes are another. Sure, failure has its place in the learning process, but there's no excuse for carelessness.

Experimentation needs focus. Improvisation should stay within certain defined boundaries. Risks should be understood, respected, and well managed. So remember—random creativity won't cut it.

Like the Pathfinder team, you need to focus your creative efforts on engineering risk out of the equation. You should reach for innovative ideas, but make sure they measurably improve the odds for overall success.

BRIAN: We were very performance-oriented. If somebody was doing the job, that's all that mattered. We didn't care if you had two years of experience or twenty.

The team did look fairly young. All the flight directors, the people responsible for operating the spacecraft in flight, were less than 40 years old. Most were under 30. Someone sent us a cartoon showing a gang of kids—scruffy-looking kids—stopped by a guard at the door to Mission Control. He's telling them, "No, you can't come in here." And they say, "But we're the flight team!"

Regardless of experience or age, we demanded performance. Quality output. The culture was one in which everybody recognized that their contribution was mission-critical. We had extremely high standards. Everybody had to take responsibility for their part of the mission. Everyone felt a very strong sense of personal ownership and commitment to their part of the job.

If there was somebody who wasn't technically competent, or maybe they just weren't motivated or weren't a team player, they didn't last very long on Pathfinder. Letting go of people is never easy and sometimes can be perceived as a little brutal. But almost without exception, when we let somebody go who wasn't doing the job or contributing to the team effort, other people came up and said, "I'm really glad you did that."

Out of all the people working on the team, over 20 were let go from the project and went elsewhere at JPL. And it was in different phases, too—a number of people in the beginning, and others at different times. It's never easy to do. But people recognize when there is something—almost like a foreign body in the system—that's not performing. If you're asking for 150 percent, and some people are giving it while somebody else is not, the good performers start to question, "Why should *I* work this hard?"

It's important for the leadership to set the standard. We expected creativity, hard work, and discipline, and we modeled that behavior in our own work. We also wanted to have fun, so we joked around a lot and tried not to take ourselves too seriously. My message to leaders is to work as hard as you expect others to work. Have fun, but don't compromise when it comes to maintaining high standards of performance.

Pathfinder Team's "scruffy-looking kids" at Kennedy Space Center just prior to launch.

Sojourner ready to begin her historic exploration of Mars. The rock named Barnacle Bill is to her left and Yogi is straight ahead.

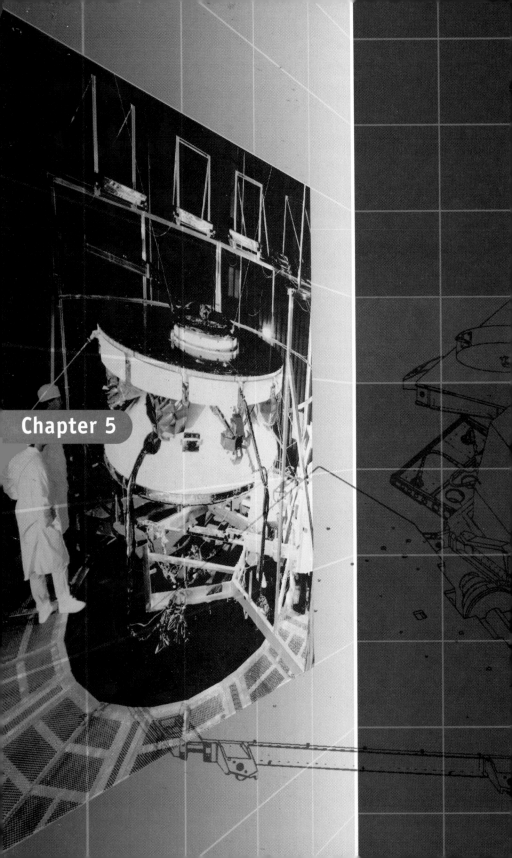

Chapter 5

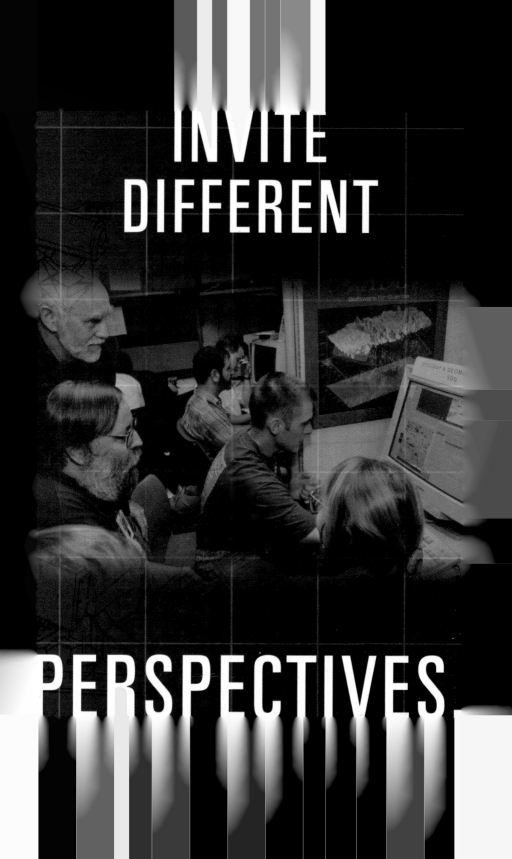

INVITE
DIFFERENT

PERSPECTIVES

Invite different perspectives.

Innovation feeds on multiple points of view. All of us can come up with original ideas on our own, but we often find more effective solutions when we also look at the situation through another person's eyes.

Nobody sees the situation exactly like you—and that's good! Everyone looks at it from a different angle. This positions them to help round out your perspective.

So call a huddle. Kick your ideas around with other people. Ask for their opinions. Bounce ideas off one another, argue about them, and watch your thoughts ricochet toward innovation.

Apply the Pathfinder technique of peer reviews—formally present your ideas to a group of knowledgeable associates, and get their critique. You'll refine your thinking through the process of preparing to teach your approach to other people. Plus, their questions and suggestions will help you shape more effective solutions.

Get input from diverse sources—people who are more experienced, less experienced, who bring different expertise, who are older or younger than you, and so on. The point is to break your established pattern of seeing and thinking. This means you need to get input from people who are outside your normal circle of friends or co-workers.

SOMEONE LIKE YOUR-DAD. just Kedding

Pay attention to how things are done in entirely different fields. Read. Listen. Watch how others operate. Pick up ideas on how these people approach their work. If you observe how they go about getting good results, you're likely to find something that you can apply to your situation.

Some people are more creative than others, but anyone you encounter might possibly be the person to spark a breakthrough idea.

BRIAN: We had a good mix of scarred veterans and young, relatively inexperienced people working on Pathfinder. But the bias was definitely on the younger side. People came because they heard we were going to do things differently. And they sensed an opportunity to do something special. The key was to turn this disparate group into a whole that was greater than the sum of its parts.

A lot of creative energy came from the mix of talents—the different people, in close proximity, who every day were working together, talking together, and sharing each other's problems and ideas. There's a real value associated with this mix of multi-discipline people. A hardware person thinks in terms of hardware functions. A software person thinks differently, as does a systems person. Generalists and specialists also have very different views. But by co-locating these very different disciplines—or bringing them together in meetings—something special happened. People talked to each other, learned what the other person did, and discovered they could help one another.

We also brought in people from outside the team who further rounded out our perspective. For example, we did a lot of reviews. In fact, we did over 100 peer reviews where we invited in hands-on people with current technical skills to sit in judgment of our ideas. To get ready for these reviews, we had to prepare material as if we were going to teach it. We had to explain what we were doing in great detail to people who were our peers. Nothing clarifies your understanding of your design, its strengths, and its problems like preparing for and conducting a good peer review.

Just preparing for a review gets you 90 percent of the value. Then, when you actually present the material, you get the rest of the payoff. Other people's experience comes into play, and they start questioning things and giving inputs. You get this cycle of, "Have you thought about this? What happens if this happens? That looks pretty good." Leading to, "I can change that. I can fix that. I think I'll do something different here." In the end, out of that exchange come some better ideas and confirmation that you have a sound approach. The whole intent is to end up with the features and functionality you want the first time, so you don't have to go back and fix it later on.

Generally, reviews are considered a burden, a pain. But we made them part of our culture, and people didn't object to them. It's important that these reviews were done in a non-threatening, non-competitive manner. Nobody said things like, "That's a stupid idea."

We called these peer reviews down on ourselves. People either knew or learned that these critiques could be a big help. We joked about calling in "friendly fire." But we always came out of the reviews with either a better design or more confidence that the proposed design would survive the rigors of upcoming tests and the real mission.

We also worked very closely with our vendors, national laboratories, and other NASA centers, and relied on their inputs and products. We actively worked on innovating together. Our suppliers were part of the team...part of the family. They knew that we were operating with fixed-dollar constraints. We made that clear to them. So they got creative about how they could develop their designs while controlling their costs. The vendors knew, like we at JPL did, that any of us could blow the mission. If anyone's designs weren't robust, or if any of us lost control of the development and let costs or schedules go through the roof, we were all sunk. For the people outside JPL, the shared knowledge of the constraints and being treated like full partners helped create the commitment that was essential to mission success.

There isn't always safety in numbers: Pathfinder's comparatively tiny team of only 200 was picked for its mix of scarred veterans and young, relatively inexperienced talent. (Not all shown here)

Plan...
and improvise.

Chapter 6

Perched atop the lander, the Imager
for Mars Pathfinder (IMP) returned
150 small frames that were
mosaiced into this first panoramic
view of the landing site.

Plan...and improvise.

Pathfinder used a double-barreled approach to innovate its way toward "faster-better-cheaper." On one hand, the situation called for careful preparation. On the other, it required a willingness to improvise.

In your own pursuit of spectacular results, start out by doing some "deep planning." Anticipate as best you can. Consider different scenarios, and run your calculations. Make your very best guess about how the situation will unfold. But then be willing to bob and weave.

When your plan has a hole in it or fizzles out on you, don't freeze up. Remain limber and loose. Feel your way along. Even though you may feel lost, good planning will still be serving you. It guides you invisibly when you have to operate intuitively. So press on. Mobility is crucial. Continue to actively pursue your objectives. Don't stop just because you're in uncharted territory.

You should understand, right now, that your planning is doomed in certain respects. Don't expect it to cover all contingencies, no matter how thorough you've been. It's been said that, "No plan survives contact with the enemy." In this case the "enemy" is the unknown, the unpredictable part of the future. But a key benefit of good planning is that it mentally prepares you to improvise.

In-depth planning at the outset helps you figure out what you don't know. It points to those unmapped areas where you'll have to play it by ear. In the final analysis, skillful improvisation may account for your success more than the efforts you put into crafting your approach. So be willing to change, or even abandon, your blueprint for action. The intent should be to adapt to the circumstances you encounter, not to slavishly follow an obsolete plan.

But one final point—don't get lazy about planning. A lot of people just make a superficial pass at it, counting on their quick wits and flexibility to get them by. Their so-called plan amounts to little more than deciding to wing it all the way. Don't kid yourself. The better job you do in planning, the more effective you'll be in improvising.

BRIAN: Some of the engineers at the Jet Propulsion Laboratory joke that JPL stands for "just plain lucky." But the success of Pathfinder suggests that this "luck" is the result of planning, attention to detail, thorough testing, and adapting to changes quickly and correctly. I was told that a Caltech professor had a good definition of luck. He said, "Luck is being pretty close to right." I agree with him.

It was very important to have good plans, a good sense of what we were trying to do. We knew when certain things had to be done, but there were always problems that we had to react to. Sometimes they were small and took very little corrective action. But sometimes they were major, and we had to rethink the whole flow of events. This happened particularly often during the system assembly and test activity leading up to launch.

We also had to invent a lot of things. The key to inventing on a schedule is having the plan in the back of your mind, yet being willing and able to make necessary changes quickly. We didn't fall in love with the plan and follow it blindly. If it was wrong, we changed it.

One of the best examples of planning and improvising can be seen in our preparations for operating the lander and rover on the surface of Mars. Richard Cook, the mission manager, was responsible for the surface operations plan and its execution. Practically every minute of the landing day's activities had to be planned out in great detail. We simulated the entire entry condition and the landing. And then all the operations on the surface. That helped develop our skills, our intuition, and the team dynamic. We developed a shared sense of how the group was going to work together, who was going to make the time-critical decisions, and where the crises were most likely to occur. We did cases where we went outside the expected envelope...we pushed our spacecraft and ourselves to the edge. We needed to be sure we were as ready for the unexpected as we could be.

There were so many unknowns—scenarios we could hardly imagine, let alone test. But because we planned very carefully, everyone understood what the goals were and what their role was. We knew what contingencies we had planned for, and we tested them thoroughly. These tests were done over and over again to get us ready. We tested the nominal scenarios. Then we tested off-nominally. We verified that the system would work even if certain components failed. But still we knew something, maybe many things, would be different when we actually got to the surface of Mars.

To help us test, we built a giant sandbox with sand and rocks to simulate the Mars terrain, based on what the Viking mission data led us to believe about the planet's surface. This was our testing ground for the hardware and software of the Mars lander and rover. Dave Gruel, a 27-year old engineer, was assigned to be the project's "gremlin." He got this nickname because he was our official troublemaker. He set up problem situations in the sandbox that the team had to figure out how to overcome. Behind closed doors, the gremlin would set up pathological cases in which the lander would be oriented in a very unusual way. Or he would set up the airbags or rocks in a way to impede the rover's egress from the lander. Then we would go through these tests just like it was the 4th of July. We would do our simulated landing at 10:07 a.m. and go around the clock, twenty-four hours per day for five days straight. We would have to interpret, resolve, and then fix what we saw there, all the while working to meet the mission objectives of returning pictures and delivering the rover to interesting rocks.

The value of this planning and testing showed up on the first day on Mars. One of the problem scenarios the gremlin had posed for us had the airbags draped over the lander petal, preventing the rover from driving off. We'd figured out how to fix that problem in our earth-bound sandbox by lifting up a petal and pulling the airbag in further. When we saw this same problem in our first images from Mars, we knew exactly how to handle it. Our planning and preparations had paid off, as they did a number of other times during those first few days on Mars.

Rover Driver Brian Cooper, navigating the Sojourner Rover to its next encounter with a Mars rock.

embrace

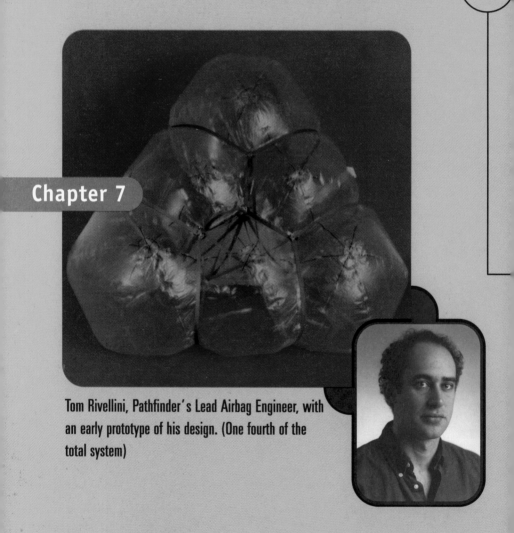

Tom Rivellini, Pathfinder's Lead Airbag Engineer, with an early prototype of his design. (One fourth of the total system)

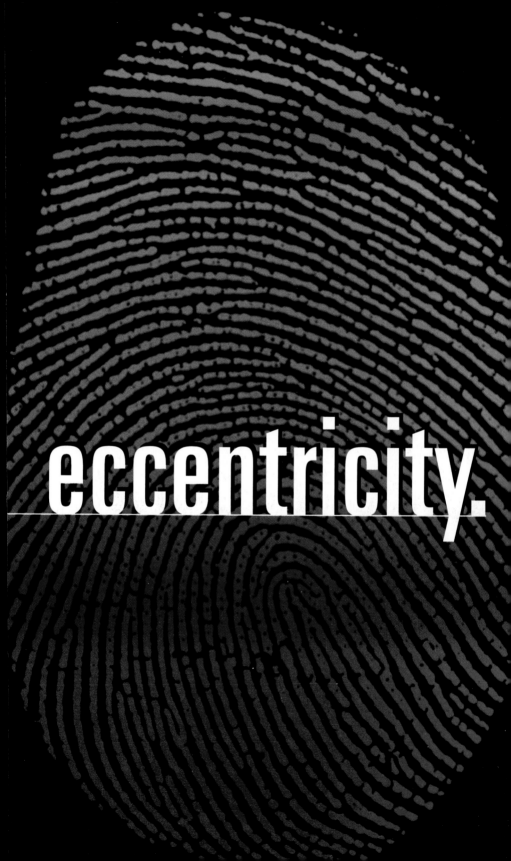

eccentricity.

Embrace eccentricity.

Now's the time to release the renegade inside.

Go to an extreme. Give yourself permission—no, an order—to reach beyond the conventional approach. Don't allow your thinking to land on the predictable solution. Reach out there! It needs to be novel.

Unless it's unusual, it's not an innovation. And if you're not innovating, you cripple your chances for achieving "faster-better-cheaper."

So raise some people's eyebrows. Let the traditionalists squirm. Maybe it's good if they begin to tut-tut your ideas or technique. If they're smirking at your "harebrained" schemes, that's probably a good sign. It lets you know you've moved beyond the boundaries of "ordinary." You're into a new zone that hasn't been milked of its innovative potential.

You've got to be willing to look a little silly, to be seen as outrageous, offbeat, or downright odd.

Defenders of the status quo won't be very kind to you, and they certainly can't be counted on for support. So don't look to them for approval. They're not into quirky or eccentric. It makes them uneasy, so they tend to put it down in one way or another. They may say you're naïve. Unscientific. Just inexperienced, or maybe even dangerous. That's okay, as long as your efforts produce the desired results.

Now the idea is not to be offbeat or eccentric just for the sake of being different. The point is to permit yourself to be a maverick if it enables you to add real value. It's all about turning yourself loose, getting really original, because it will allow you to make a valuable difference. But that difference must be viable…commercial…something that works.

If eccentricity helps you achieve the intended goal, and if you produce within the boundary lines set for the task, it passes the legitimacy test.

BRIAN: We came up with two basic concepts for landing Pathfinder on the surface of Mars. One was a traditional approach—propulsive descent—just like Viking had done in 1976. The other concept was a wild idea—using giant airbags to cushion the lander's impact, then letting it bounce and roll to a stop.

NASA basically looked at the two options and said, "Well, propulsion…that's the old way of doing business. You guys will never get this job done if you do it that way. It's too expensive." And so we said, "Okay, let's go make this airbag thing work."

The airbags idea was clearly eccentric. Off the charts. When you think of an airbag, you think of the automobile design, about twice the size of a pillow, which took many years to develop. But what we needed would have to be about 19 feet in diameter, designed to tolerate a head-on collision with a very rocky Mars surface at 60 miles per hour or more. And not just once, but multiple times, as it bounced and rolled to a stop. The only thing common between our design and an automobile airbag was the name. Another very eccentric aspect of this was the idea of using fabrics in outer space. We were used to dealing in aluminum and titanium, but this needed to be the stuff of bulletproof vests…advanced polymer cloth. We'd worked with software in space, but not "softgoods."

The young man who had come up with the kernel of the airbag concept was Tomasso Rivellini. Tom had never done a flight hardware engineering job before, but he had the right energy and creative instincts. So we gave him the job. Of course, he knew he needed help. He went to Bob Bamford and Bill Layman, two of JPL's intellectual giants, for help in developing the basic design. But once Tom started working the details, he alone was responsible for figuring out a way to build and test this behemoth. Tom knew that JPL didn't have the expertise in working with fabrics and

Pathfinder's airbag system, poised here for drop-testing onto a rock-strewn platform raised 60 ft. in the air. More than 20 such tests were conducted to develop and verify the airbag design.

sewing—with so-called "softgoods." So he sought out and found people at Sandia National Laboratory in Albuquerque and ILC Dover in Dover, Delaware, to help build a scale model followed by full-scale prototypes. This job took a lot of trial and error. Tom started with a 1/20th scale model, and worked up to full scale. It turned out that the only way to really understand how an airbag works is to test it full scale.

Every time we showed the video of the first full-scale test, in which the airbags were dropped about 120 ft. onto a flat surface, people laughed. It did look comical seeing a giant beachball bounce like a superball. But our early attempts were

Full-scale airbags, approximately 19 ft. in height, being readied for testing in JPL's "Mars Yard."

discouraging. Our first drops on a rocky surface simulating expected Martian terrain were complete failures. We weren't sure if this thing was going to work. But we kept working the details, improving the design, and going back into test. It was a very iterative process. We tried an analytical approach, but we spent over a week of Cray computer time to get only a few seconds of data on the impact. The problem was just too complex for state-of-the-art analysis tools at that time. So we had to rely on Tom and his team's ability to design, build, and test their way to a design that would work. And they did.

The manager of NASA's Viking mission to Mars—the legendary Jim Martin—was, at best, skeptical that the airbag idea would work. He chaired the formal review boards that oversaw the project's progress throughout its three-year development. He knew about all the trials and tribulations of the airbag development, and that the proof would only come on landing day. On July 4th, 1997, Jim and I were standing next to each other shortly after the landing. Jim turned to me and said, "You know, Brian, I think these airbags ought to be the required technology, the technology of choice, for any mission that is going to land where the terrain is unknown." Our eccentric idea had just become mainstream.

Proceed with optimism

Leaving a Legacy: On a tiny piece of silicon were etched
the names of thousands of participants and supporters of
the Mars Pathfinder Project. The silicon chip was attached
to the lander just before launch.

Chapter 8

and a "can-do spirit."

One young, aspiring astronaut's rendering of the rover.

Proceed with optimism and a "can-do spirit."

Innovation comes easier when we carry ourselves with the right kind of attitude. If our mental set includes confidence, optimism, and possibility thinking, we're bound to become more open-minded to opportunity.

An upbeat outlook like this provides an emotional foundation for belief. It carries a person forward, supplying the emotional strength to take risks. To experiment. And to persevere. With this sturdy faith that a solution exists, and can be found, we readily go exploring.

The "can-do spirit" is a mindset that sustains. This kind of thinking produces a mental toughness that enables us to press on through failure, to see it as part of the learning process and not as a final result. Practice this kind of attitude, and you'll hang tough in the face of problems and disappointments. You'll be able to keep the faith through criticism and your own confusion.

This is an outlook that can be learned, a perspective on the world that can be practiced and developed. To exercise these muscles in your mind, just follow the advice of Dorothea Brande, who said, "Act as if it were impossible to fail." Simple enough. Just press on, behaving

the way you surely would if you knew success could be yours by

persevering.

When our actions are guided and energized by certainty that we will

prevail, we liberate ourselves. The mighty power of our instincts and

intuition are released, magnifying our effectiveness as human beings.

Blessed are the believers, for they shall be better equipped to innovate.

I couldn't find it in my Bible, the way
they wrote it here. But in my Bible
it say I know in whom I have believe
and I know that greater is he that is
in me. And I can do all things
thur Him.

BRIAN: Working on Pathfinder felt like a roller coaster ride. Sometimes you were up, sometimes down. These highs and lows came and went on a daily basis. For me sometimes it was hourly. But it was particularly important for me to maintain a confident attitude, because people always look to the leader for a sign of how things are going. If the boss thinks things are impossible, then the battle is already lost.

There were many times when very tough problems showed up. Real challenges, possible show stoppers. But without exception, the team would rise to the occasion. You could see their motivation, their enthusiasm. They were not going to give up.

One of the subsystems that really struggled on its own roller coaster ride was the telecommunications system, which is a fancy word for the radio and antennae. And in the case of deep space radios, which must work reliably over millions of miles, they are fancy things indeed.

The Pathfinder telecommunications system was one of the highest technology subsystems on the spacecraft. Practically every part had a major element of brand-new technology. Typically, building and testing a new radio system is one of the most challenging, high-risk parts of spacecraft development. It always requires great skill and attention to detail. Unfortunately, during the course of the design, the leader of the telecommunications system team suddenly left JPL. We were in a crisis situation. We had lots of technical problems and no leader.

That's when Leslie Livesay entered the picture. She was one of only a few people at JPL with the experience and skill to complete such a complex system on a near impossible schedule. Leslie walked into a situation where every time she turned over a rock there was a snake. It was not clear whether their team would make it at all, let alone on the original schedule. But Leslie literally rolled up her sleeves and, shoulder-to-shoulder with her team, put the radio electronics together and fully tested it in record time. She set the tone. She stated and showed her confidence that the job could be done. Along with her team, she put in the time and effort it took to get their subsystem delivered on schedule.

The Pathfinder telecommunications system worked flawlessly throughout the mission. Leslie was in the mission control room the morning of July 4th. She'd told me that if Pathfinder got down to the surface of Mars, her radio would successfully transmit the message to the world.

And it did.

The lander and rover ready for testing in JPL's "space simulator" chamber.

Leslie Livesay, telecommunications lead engineer, monitoring testing of Pathfinder radio performance.

The success of the Pathfinder mission is another addition to the lore that is part of JPL's culture. We've done a lot of jobs that at first seemed near impossible, starting with the first spacecraft ever launched by the United States—Explorer I. It was built in just four months and launched successfully in 1958. JPL has developed an attitude that is experience-based, a confidence that comes from seeing what people can do in the face of seemingly impossible odds.

Develop robust solutions.

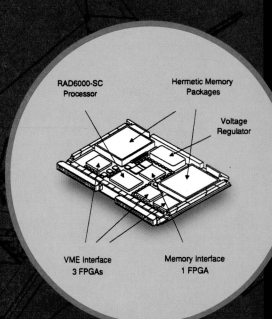

Chapter 9

RAD6000-SC
Processor

Hermetic Memory
Packages

Voltage
Regulator

VME Interface
3 FPGAs

Memory Interface
1 FPGA

The 1/2" x 1/2" microprocessor that was the sole computer brain of the Pathfinder lander.

Develop robust solutions.

The Pathfinder mission to Mars was not a reckless project. When all was said and done, there was an unbending end-game accountability. The only acceptable outcome was success—that meant Mars...on time, on budget.

The JPL team's instructions were clear: "Take risks, but don't fail." This meant they were expected to be innovative, but with a keen attention to risk management. Their response was to "build in margin," crafting solutions that were very robust in the sense that they were "tolerant to the uncertainties." This line of thinking says you can go with far-out solutions if you've factored in enough of a safety zone.

Robust solutions come from exposing your ideas to relentless testing. Constant critique. The idea is to make smart mistakes—that is, make your mistakes early on, and capture the learning that occurs.

Ask other people to create roadblocks on purpose, and see if your solutions can measure up. This kind of action-oriented research finds your soft spots, the vulnerable points that need to be improved for your innovations to succeed in the real world. By subjecting your solutions to intense scrutiny, you're able to take out much of the risk at the front end.

What this comes down to could be called "engineered luck." The intensive testing doesn't guarantee a perfect solution, but promises that you will be as prepared as you can. Robust solutions are smart, informed approaches. They have built-in backup to compensate for the weaker aspects of your solution, and extra padding to protect you from the unknowns.

The lesson here is to take risks. But do the testing, and build in the margin necessary to protect you against the unknowns you may encounter.

BRIAN: We faced a lot of unknowns in getting to Mars and exploring its surface terrain. We had developed the most complete understanding possible of the conditions we would face. But just like the weather, we could have been very badly surprised. That was one of our biggest nightmares. We had designed Pathfinder for a certain environment—a very challenging one—but if the environment was significantly different, was the design robust enough to survive it?

Robustness and demonstrated margin were key to the success of a design that was basically single-string. For most elements of the spacecraft, we were one resistor, one transistor, one integrated circuit, one mechanical device away from potential disaster. And so to make sure we didn't have a disaster, we tested the hell out of every part of the spacecraft.

Robustness means there's a lot of margin—a lot of tolerance to changes, miscalculations, or new environments. Robustness can save you when the uncertainties, the "unknown-unknowns," suddenly become known. Bill Layman, the mechanical subsystems chief engineer and veteran of many JPL missions, taught me, "Kill it with margin. If you can, put in enough margin so that you don't have to think about it again." It's a very effective way of managing risk, if you can afford it.

We strove to put lots of margin in the entry, descent, and landing design early. Rob Manning, Dara Sabahi, and Sam Thurman were the leaders of the entry, descent, and landing design. They put their design through a lot of unusual test cases and it kept working. But they never quit trying to make it more robust. Nobody ever stopped and said, "Well, that's good enough." There was always a sense of, "Can I make this even better? Is there something else I can do, some other test we can run, to increase the likelihood of success?"

But sometimes adding robustness can look risky itself. As the parachute and airbag designs were developing, it became clear that if the lander got much heavier the parachute would not be able to slow the lander down enough for the airbag to work reliably. We felt that the airbag could only handle about a 60 mph impact, but it looked like the parachute couldn't slow us down that much if the lander got too heavy. It was my judgment and experience that the lander would get heavier as its design matured. So the question was should I gamble that it wouldn't grow too much and that we'd still make it, or should we try to "kill it"? We decided to kill the problem by adding a rocket deceleration system that would slow the lander down just before impact. This was a whole new subsystem for the entry, descent, and landing phase—three solid rockets. We caught a lot of criticism for adding this element to an already complex system. But as the mass of the lander grew (well beyond my earliest estimates), the rocket system provided all the margin we needed to keep within the performance range of the airbags. In the end, it turned out that the

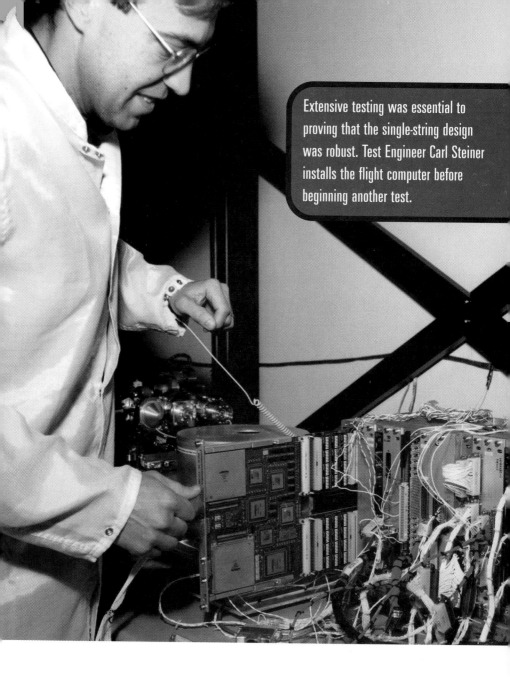

Extensive testing was essential to proving that the single-string design was robust. Test Engineer Carl Steiner installs the flight computer before beginning another test.

slowest speed the parachute could provide by itself was 140 mph, way beyond the capability of the airbag. Adding the rocket system provided robustness early in the design. This allowed us to proceed confidently with the parachute and airbag designs, saving us time and money. In the end, the rocket system actually reduced our overall risks and was a major contributor to the success of the mission.

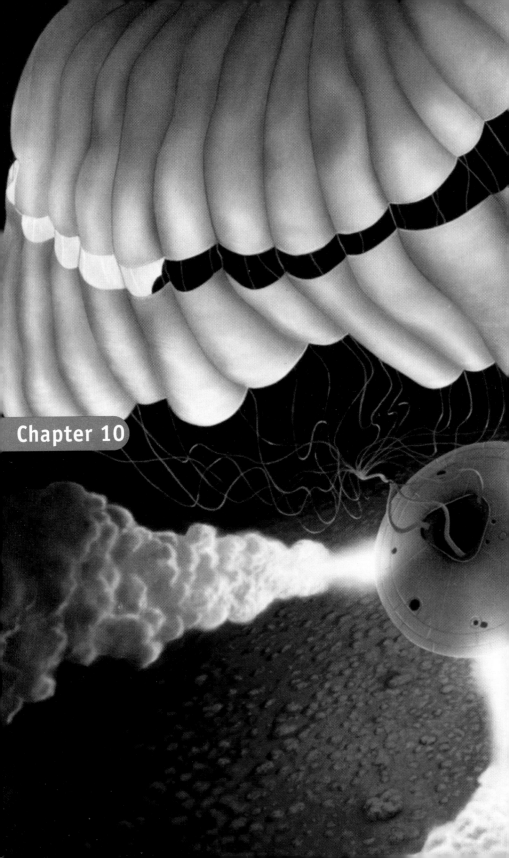

Chapter 10

Maintain momentum
and *forward* motion.

Maintain momentum and forward motion.

"Faster-better-cheaper," by definition, calls for an aggressive approach... a relentless push for progress. JPL's Mars Pathfinder team achieved its spectacular results by pressing forward and steadily covering ground.

This kind of approach is crucial, because movement accelerates the discovery process. It takes us toward solutions, teaches us, and makes the most of our precious time. These benefits argue for a bias toward action and suggest we should operate with a sense of urgency.

Momentum stands as a high priority because schedule slippages carry such heavy costs. In particular, they waste time, a precious and irreplaceable resource. Idling down also causes us to learn more slowly, miss opportunities, and burn up more energy getting started again. We should stay on the go, rather than allowing the organization's metabolism to get sluggish.

Today's innovation needs to take place in real time. The competitive atmosphere is too intense for a slow-paced creative process to serve an organization well. So we must innovate on the fly, doing it as we go instead of trying to figure out everything before we go. More than ever before, we must rely on action to be our educator.

Constant pursuit of our objective is important if we want to accomplish things quicker…if we want to maintain momentum…if we are uncertain, confused, or need answers. Overall, forward motion is the most informative and innovation-friendly behavior you can find.

The secret is to stay on the offensive. To keep moving and push ahead. This actually forces us to be more innovative, just as it helps us hold our speed.

Final verification test of retro-rocket system at China Lake Naval Weapons Center, California.

BRIAN: A lot of people would have given you very good odds that Pathfinder wouldn't even make it to the launch pad, let alone to the surface of Mars. One of the things that was essential to our success was maintaining momentum. We had a short time frame. We had a lot to do. So we had to keep moving, making a lot of decisions based on scarce or limited information, and cranking in course corrections as we learned more.

About a year from launch, we were out in the California desert conducting what we thought would be the final verification test of the rocket-assisted deceleration system. We were looking at the initial test results, and everything looked fine. Then, on a closer look we discovered an anomaly. There was an instability in the way the rocket burned. This was totally unexpected, and it changed our whole outlook on how the system might perform. This instability changed the thrust profile of the engine. That could significantly degrade our ability to stop at the right time during descent and could jeopardize the airbag's ability to land safely.

All we knew was that the test structure was not like the flight backshell (the structure that supports the engines when they fire), and that aluminum in the rocket propellant helps stabilize the motor's burning. There was no textbook answer to this problem. We consulted with the best experts in the field and there was no clear answer as to the cause. But they did have some theories. This was a case of, "Am I going to study this some more? Generate a few Ph.D. dissertations? Risk running out of time? Or just try to kill it?"

We could study the problem some more or we could go with the most plausible theory, use our best judgment, and go test it. The plausible theory pointed to the aluminum in the propellant. We had taken almost all of it out in order to reduce the likelihood of contaminating the surfaces we wanted to analyze. So in a matter of three days we consulted the experts, the manufacturer, and the science team. Then I made the decision. Put all the aluminum back in the engines. Remake all the engines, and then retest them in the flight configuration using the engineering model backshell (almost identical to the flight backshell). This was a bold plan. If it worked we were home free, if it didn't we'd miss the launch. But at the same time, if we didn't move out quickly toward this potential solution we'd also miss the launch. So off we went at full speed, knowing that the proof would be in the final test.

The new engines were built and the final test was completed just six months before launch. The test was completely successful. The speed with which we'd evaluated the problem, implemented the solution, and verified it was typical of the way things got done on Pathfinder.

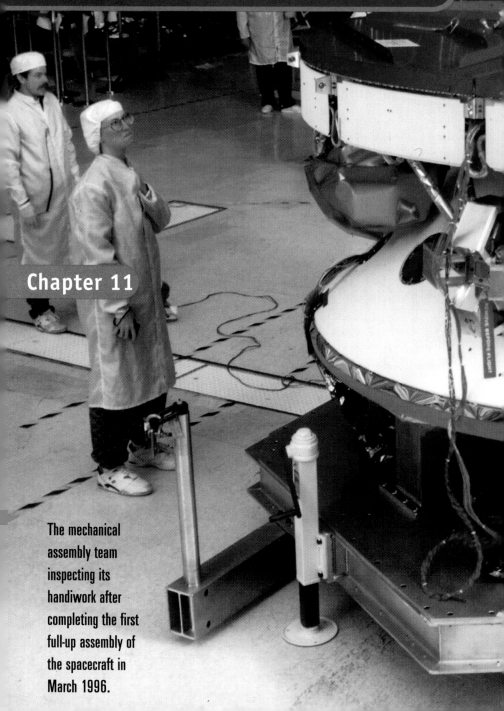

Be fully trustworthy.

Chapter 11

The mechanical assembly team inspecting its handiwork after completing the first full-up assembly of the spacecraft in March 1996.

We can't expect to achieve at the Pathfinder level without special effort. It takes a very effective team. And whether it's stated or unstated, such high-performance work groups operate according to a pretty clear code of conduct. Everyone is expected to help create and maintain a climate of trust.

This calls for mutual respect, and that requires each individual to be fully competent in his or her domain. In other words, your performance must be "worth trusting." The rest of the group has got to be able to count on you—not just to rely on you to do your work well, but also to be there when teammates need backup. You're "mission critical." Your results matter, and so do you.

The methods you use to get those results matter as well. Trust hinges on openness and honesty, on one's personal integrity. This means keeping your word, meeting your commitments, and going public if you need help or make mistakes. One of the worst things you can do is hide problems or try to cover up your errors. Surface them. See that they get resolved, because they can make the difference between mission success or failure. Problem identification and resolution serve as vehicles for learning. They can educate everyone on how to deal with the circumstances in question.

The trust level plays a crucial role in high-performance organizations. Everybody doesn't have to agree all the time, but you need mutual respect. It's also important for you to trust one another's word. If we want people to be collaborative, they need to be comfortable with one another's character and competence. If risk-taking and innovation are important, people must feel that it's safe to take an intelligent gamble.

So day in, day out, take responsibility for building and maintaining the character of your team.

BRIAN: The JPL culture I grew up in was one where everybody understood the criticality of their job.

Like most companies, we do as much as we can to build in checks and balances to try to identify mistakes and potential problems early. But any such system is imperfect, and ultimately it comes down to the fact that there are always going to be things that only a single individual knows. One person who fails to identify a problem or is inattentive to a critical detail can take down the whole mission. And everybody knows it.

You can't build in enough checks and balances to catch everything. So it's up to the integrity of each individual to ensure that their hardware and/or software will do what it needs to do when tested against the rigors of space. The working team has to trust that they can bring a problem to the managers without getting their heads taken off. And management has to have people that they can trust, people to whom they can give the responsibility and authority to make things happen.

On Pathfinder we created an atmosphere of integrity and trust that started with the project leaders. Beginning with the Project Manager, Tony Spear, we set the tone by working openly and honestly with each other. Everybody operated with a high level of integrity, and we checked our egos at the door. This spirit was infectious and it permeated the whole team. There was trust and respect both ways, up and down the team. It was rare, but if someone turned out not to be trustworthy, they didn't last long on the Pathfinder team.

One of my favorite examples of an individual's integrity came during one of the final checkovers of the spacecraft just weeks before launch. One of the spacecraft assembly technicians—Larry Broms—thought he had seen something incorrect in how a cable had been routed through a cable cutter. This cable was at risk of being prematurely cut if not properly installed. Although this was not his area of responsibility, he brought it to the attention of the engineer leading the assembly. All the paperwork said the job had been done right, but Larry held his ground. When they looked closer, they discovered that Larry was right. We spent a little while trying to figure out how the mistake was made. Then we removed the assembly and fixed it. If Larry had not caught the mistake and taken responsibility for making sure it was right, it could have resulted in mission failure. This kind of integrity and commitment was essential to the success of Mars Pathfinder.

Rover engineers performing final inspection of Sojourner
at Kennedy Space Center prior to mounting on lander.

An early eight-wheel rover design
tickles kids' fancy.

Take personal responsibility

Chapter 12

for communication.

"Faster-better-cheaper" uses information exchange as its motor. It requires tight coordination. Effective linkages. A free flow of ideas. Information hoarding is a cardinal sin and openness a key virtue.

That's because communication problems never remain just communication problems. They weaken everything else. If you let communications get balled up, performance goes down. If people fall into the habit of hiding problems, sitting on good ideas, or withholding information, you soon end up with "slower-worse-more expensive."

Nevertheless, an attitude still lingering in the minds of some people says, "If the people in charge want me to know, they'll come and tell me. If there's a problem, somebody else will fix it. If I've got a good idea, I'm gonna keep it to myself." This kills an organization's innovative potential. Each person needs to take responsibility for seeking understanding. This means actively chasing down the answers we need. Attacking problems. And if we know of information that should be communicated to others, our job is to push it through the pipeline to them.

The hairier the issues, the more important it is that they be identified and confronted. They belong in the communication loop. So don't dodge the sensitive stuff. Deal with it—keep it on the table until the people involved have worked it through. The idea is to be hard on the issues, soft on the people. That protects the relationships that are involved, yet allows you to get to the guts of the problem.

High-quality communication doesn't come easy, and hardly ever occurs by accident. It requires personal attention. It takes a lot of time. But it's absolutely essential in today's real-time environment.

BRIAN: JPL sometimes is a little bit like a medieval society. The story goes like this. Once upon a time, there were two very important fiefdoms. One controlled the land of spacecraft attitude control (the electronics and software that govern the way the spacecraft flies in space). The other controlled the land of command and data (controlling the flow of information to and from the Earth). Together they basically control most of what happens on a spacecraft.

Typically, those two fiefdoms are completely autonomous. They have their own hardware, their own computers, their own software. This is a good arrangement for the fiefdoms, but not optimum for the kingdom. So one day the king (the project) decided to marry together the fiefdoms that supported Pathfinder. It would be a shotgun wedding. And to assure its success, we co-located the newlyweds together…right outside my office door.

This marriage was driven by the need to do things faster, better, and cheaper. Since there was fundamentally no difference in the technology the two groups used, I knew the marriage should be easy. It was just the attitudes of the management that needed to be overcome. By co-locating the two groups with the project, we not only eliminated the management rivalry, but also discovered that we had stumbled onto a boon to communications, creativity, and productivity.

A great example of how co-location enhanced productivity came from one of the software engineers, David Smyth, who was working on a special piece of software. He needed a way to make something happen at a particular time. That can be hard to do sometimes in software, and he was having a difficult time. Just across the wall from him was a hardware guy designing the chip David was trying to control. Since David had met this hardware guy and knew what he was working on, he just went around the corner and asked, "Hey, Chris, can you give me a trigger—a timer—in your hardware that will allow me to time my software?" And Chris said, "No problem." They worked out the details and the hardware change was made in minutes. This brief conversation saved hours of software work and probably days of testing.

That kind of breakthrough simply would not have happened if these two guys had not been co-located. It was a case where two working-level engineers from completely different disciplines took the initiative to make a system-level improvement. They didn't have to ask anybody's permission. They just took responsibility for doing what made sense.

We used all forms of electronic information exchange, especially email and voicemail. It all helped, but something special happens with face-to-face communication. Chance encounters while just walking down the halls often

Deep Space Network Tracking Station at Tidbinbilla, Australia (near Canberra), one of the three sites located around the globe to maintain continuous communications with deep space probes.

The landing day press conference with Muirhead explaining the landing status.

resulted in valuable insights. I'd ask how things were going, and someone would launch into a story about a potential problem I hadn't heard about yet. There were a lot of times when an encounter would turn into a problem-solving session and we'd make a decision right there in the hall. Too often people hold issues or information until the next staff meeting or until they can get on the decision-maker's calendar. But when you see the boss right outside your office, it's a great opportunity to make something happen immediately.

Good communications and co-location also build teams. An atmosphere of open communication and shared space helps build human relationships. Just by seeing each other every day, you learn people's names, you go and have lunch, and opportunities for creativity and enhanced productivity just happen. Also, if everybody is pretty much interconnected, then problems don't get a chance to get very big without somebody else knowing about it.

Chapter 13

Demonstrate passionate

The first image of Mars taken from the lander.

commitment to success.

The second Mars image.

Demonstrate passionate commitment to success.

The innovations that are involved in achieving "faster-better-cheaper" come through people. Human beings serve as the most important hardware in the creative process. The most important software, however, is the programming found in people's hearts and minds.

If we're emotionally flat or intellectually uninspired, innovation keeps its distance. Failure prowls around the edges of our efforts. Success doesn't like to show its face. Those things that do get accomplished carry the stamp of mediocrity, and give us no real sense of accomplishment.

Let's contrast the results of those lukewarm efforts with what happens when we're passionately committed to success...when the emotional investment in our work rises far above room temperature.

In those situations where our heart gets involved in the effort—where we care fiercely about the outcomes—a "give what it takes" attitude takes over. We tackle assignments with an unyielding determination that simply refuses to accept defeat. We willingly make personal sacrifices, putting in long hours and hard work. If our hearts are set on the team's success, we operate from a systems viewpoint. This encourages us to look beyond the boundaries of our immediate responsibilities to consider the needs of the overall effort. And we pitch in to help others without hesitation.

People who are hell-bent on achieving their objectives have a personal intensity that's contagious. It inspires others to outdo themselves. This passion brings out everybody's best, and the whole becomes much greater than the sum of its parts.

What this means is that you need to go far past the point of merely being responsible. We're not talking here about simply having good work habits. And this isn't about how many brain cells you've got engaged. It's about having fire inside, a vitality born of being emotionally married to the idea of accomplishing your goal.

Bottom line, it's a statement about you, a naked indicator of how much heart and soul you're investing. It signals whether your creative spirit has been stirred, whether the explorer within you has awakened, and whether you've tapped into that great potential you have inside.

BRIAN: One of the last things we can define, and one of the very first things that is needed to start a spacecraft assembly, is the electrical interconnect hardware—the wiring. We call it cabling. Normally it's thought of as a fairly mundane item because it's relatively low-tech. But it's absolutely critical. Without it, nothing can get started.

The people who do the cabling on a spacecraft are always caught in a tight squeeze between the time the cabling is defined and the time it's needed. That was particularly true on Pathfinder. As soon as we got our electrical interface defined, we started generating the cabling drawings. But the real responsibility for the build fell to a group of women in JPL's cabling shop. These women are very skilled technicians used to doing very precise hand labor. They had to make over 2,000 point-to-point electrical connections with 100% accuracy—plus they had to route and safely tie down the equivalent of more than two miles of wire throughout the spacecraft. This wiring had to survive the high "g" forces of a rocket launch as well as the impact of the landing on Mars.

This team assembled around a lead person named Linda Ponce. They developed a special camaraderie and somehow came to call themselves the Seven Dwarfs. Each of them had selected a name which fit their personalities—Linda was "Doc," and "Grumpy" was the quality assurance person. As I got to know the "Dwarfs" better, I was amazed at how well their pseudo-names fit them.

These women really pulled together under enormous pressure. They knew they were a critical delivery. To make things worse, the design kept changing, and there were last minute problems and redesigns. We ended up having to tear out a whole bunch of wiring because of engineering problems. But the "Dwarfs" kept going. At one particularly critical stage, Linda came in on Sunday just to assess the team's progress and plan the next week's activities. She did this on her own initiative, even after working six days straight.

I came down to the cable shop nearly every day, sometimes twice a day, to see how things were going and help work bottlenecks that might slow them down. As the team was struggling with the most complex harness, I made a bet with Linda, saying, "If your team can deliver this harness with three or less errors, I'll buy everyone a bottle of Tequila." "If it's Cuervo 1800, you're on," said Linda. As Linda's team finished this first build and took this octopus-like harness into test, I could see they were excited. Not about the bet, but about the fact that they had accomplished a very challenging job under a lot of pressure. After two days of testing, the results came in—three easy-to-fix errors were found. The Seven Dwarfs had won the bet, and I was very happy to pay off. I hope they enjoyed their Cuervo, because they certainly earned it.

The Seven Dwarfs (minus Grumpy) assembling Pathfinder flight wiring harness in May 1995.

You can't order that kind of commitment. You can't command it. It has to come from inside—that sense of being part of the mission, and of people knowing that their job is important.

I noticed a saying I'd never seen before over the door of a small restaurant in Florida. It read, "In the race for quality, there's never a finish line." I immediately thought of Linda and the Dwarfs.

Salute the past,
embrace the future.

If we examine the history of the human race, we see that exploration and innovation are part of our nature. We are born to discover. To create. And as the centuries have come and gone, we have demonstrated a rapidly accelerating ability to do things "faster-better-cheaper." Pathfinder is just another chapter in this great adventure story about our progress…about mankind's process of "becoming."

The JPL team's dramatic mission to Mars simply represents one more step toward our destiny. As we discover more about our universe, we discover more about ourselves—our possibilities—and we continue to extend our reach.

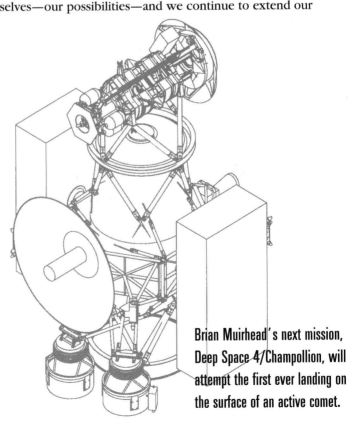

Brian Muirhead's next mission, Deep Space 4/Champollion, will attempt the first ever landing on the surface of an active comet.

"This is an exciting time to be alive, and to be explorers."
—NASA

Books by Pritchett & Associates

* *Fast Growth: A Career Acceleration Strategy*

* *Outsourced: The Employee Handbook: 12 New Rules for Running Your Career in an Interconnected World*

 Mindshift: The Employee Handbook for Understanding the Changing World of Work

* *The Employee Handbook of New Work Habits for a Radically Changing World*

* *Firing Up Commitment During Organizational Change*

 Resistance: Moving Beyond the Barriers to Change

* *Business As UnUsual: The Handbook for Managing and Supervising Organizational Change*

* *The Employee Handbook for Organizational Change*

* *Team ReConstruction: Building a High Performance Work Group During Change*

* *Teamwork: The Team Member Handbook*

* *High-Velocity Culture Change: A Handbook for Managers*

* *Culture Shift: The Employee Handbook for Changing Corporate Culture*

 The Ethics of Excellence

 A Survival Guide to the Stress of Organizational Change

* *Service Excellence!*

 Smart Moves: A Crash Course on Merger Integration Management

* *Mergers: Growth in the Fast Lane*

 The Employee Survival Guide to Mergers and Acquisitions

 After the Merger: The Authoritative Guide for Integration Success

 Making Mergers Work: A Guide to Managing Mergers and Acquisitions

 The Quantum Leap Strategy

 you^2: A High-Velocity Formula for Multiplying Your Personal Effectiveness in Quantum Leaps

New!
Thought Leader Series: Quick-Read Handbooks

* *Leadership Engine: Building Leaders at Every Level,* based on Noel Tichy and Eli Cohen's best-selling hardcover book from HarperBusiness, a division of HarperCollins Publishers.

---

* *Training program also available. Please call 1-800-992-5922 for more information.*

Call 972-789-7999 for information regarding international rights and foreign translations.

ORDER FORM

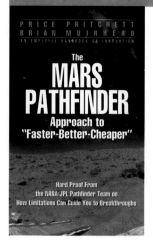

1-14 copies	____ copies at $9.95 each
15-29 copies	____ copies at $7.95 each
30-99 copies	____ copies at $5.95 each
100-999 copies	____ copies at $5.75 each
1,000-4,999 copies	____ copies at $5.50 each
5,000-9,999 copies	____ copies at $5.25 each
10,000 or more copies	____ copies at $5.00 each

Name _____

Job Title _____

Organization _____

Phone _____

Street Address _____

P.O. Box _____

City, State _____ Zip _____

Country _____

Purchase order number (if applicable) _____

Email address _____

Applicable sales tax, shipping and handling charges will be added. Prices subject to change.

Orders less than $100 require prepayment. $100 or more may be invoiced.

☐ Check Enclosed   ☐ Please Invoice

☐ **VISA**   ☐ MasterCard   ☐ AMERICAN EXPRESS

Account Number _____ Expiration Date _____

Signature _____

To order, call: 800-992-5922
fax: 972-789-7900
email: http://www.PritchettNet.com/order
or mail this form to the address below

PRITCHETT & ASSOCIATES, INC.
13155 Noel Road, Suite 1600, Dallas, Texas 75240
http://www.PritchettNet.com

KA 8399

- *Wish your teams were producing more spectacular results?*
  - *Want more good ideas turned into innovative deliverables?*
    - *Interested in learning how your organization can explore new opportunities?*

Let Pritchett & Associates run a Discovery Program in your organization. We'll help you identify a high-payoff business objective appropriate for an innovation-based Pathfinder Project. After helping you select the right members for the team, we'll train those key players on how to run a "faster-better-cheaper" project using a systems approach to project innovation. Stand back and watch as your Pathfinder Team blazes a new trail, demonstrating how the right people with the right resources can produce breakthrough results.

Our consultants will stage your Pathfinder Team for success. Then they'll coach as your team innovates its way to spectacular results. During the process, we'll be transferring our project innovation tools and techniques directly to them. They'll walk away from this project with real skills, tangible tools and practical experience using leading-edge project innovation techniques.

Everyone knows people learn more effectively by doing. Being a member of a Pathfinder Project Team lets individuals experience the dynamics of team innovation firsthand, applying what they're learning to an actual business application.

Focus your organizational energy with our Discovery Program and set your people up for "faster-better-cheaper" results.

**For more information about our Discovery Program,
call 1-800-992-5922.**

The Mars Pathfinder Video: A Story of People, Innovation and Spectacular Results

This thrilling, two-volume video presents a best practices summary of 1997's most spectacular and exciting news story on innovation: the Pathfinder mission to Mars.

Volume 1 gives a brief history of this truly inspiring accomplishment, and sets the stage to implement change in a way that energizes your organization. This volume works well as a high-impact introduction to the Mars Pathfinder mission when you're distributing this handbook to your employees. *(Length: 13 minutes)*

In *Volume 2,* Price Pritchett and Brian Muirhead draw the explosive new business messages out of the lessons learned from this mission, and demonstrate how companies can actually embed innovation in the way they operate. Pritchett and Muirhead's in-depth discussion of the six mission-critical success factors covers Clear Sense of Mission, Hands-on Leadership, Innovation, The Right Team, Trust/Openness, and Communication. Use it for a more comprehensive treatment of the issues discussed in the book. *(Length: 40 minutes)*

This powerful video set will inspire your team and provide insights into how a Pathfinder project can channel your organization's energy toward spectacular results.

Total Length: 53 minutes
$995

Pritchett Online Learning Institute

The Pritchett Online Learning Institute is a state-of-the-art extranet site providing online access to Pritchett & Associates' best-selling handbooks. These fresh, honest, pointed messages about change speak to all readers, regardless of the roles they play in your organization. The Pritchett Online Learning Institute...

- Allows instant distribution of selected handbooks and easy desktop access whenever needed.
- Provides additional products such as assessments, screensavers, and other handbooks at no extra cost.
- Allows you to review test scores, get feedback, and evaluate employees' understanding of the subject matter.

Preview the Online Institute at www.pritchettonline.com.

For more information about both products, call 1-800-992-5922